Earthquakes,
The Big Ones,
Before, During, After

Tom Willett

ISBN-10:1544939108

ISBN-13:978-1544939100

DEDICATION

Dedicated to Dave "Curlee" Williams (1913-1970).

CONTENTS

ACKNOWLEDGMENTS

Mankind has managed to make progress in understanding earthquakes and how they occur. From underground sensors to orbiting satellites information has been gathered, especially in the past few decades, which has helped make building codes more focused toward safety. Areas have been designated as "active" for tremors of high magnitude, and those areas have received very close scrutiny. Scientists have accurately predicted where earthquakes are most likely to happen. Not when, however.

Edgar Cayce, "The Sleeping Prophet," has predicted a massive California quake that will occur three months after the eruption of Mount Vesuvius or Mount Pelee. Maybe there will be a three month warning.

The USGS has predicted a 7.5 major movement in the Tejon Summit area that could stretch for many miles and last for several minutes, sometime in the next thirty years. They give it a 16% chance.

Many seers and prophets have predicted doom for Los Angeles. They could all be wrong. Los Angeles could shake for five minutes today or tomorrow or several decades from now. My prediction is simple. California is ripe for, not one, but a series of big earthquakes that will do incredible damage.

I think the crazy people who predict a Big One and the news anchors who seek safety under their desks in moderate tremors, are doing a service for those who are smart enough to prepare.

Most of what is written in this booklet is focused on the United States coming earthquakes. There have been movies about the San Andreas fault and about a big earthquake in Los Angeles. It is a good idea to watch some of those films with the knowledge that the Big One and Big Ones will happen. The soap opera that is mixed into the story is probably no more or less true than the stories of any of the families that will experience the shaking that will someday happen.

Anywhere on planet Earth there could be a dangerous natural disaster. What is written in this book and other books about earthquakes will better prepare you for whatever comes along.

I have to acknowledge the experiences of my friends who suffered damage in the 1994 Northridge quake. One of my friends lost his apartment. The building had to be torn down. He also lost his job in Northridge. His experiences made me more aware of how close we are to disaster. My next door neighbor in Van Nuys also had a major property loss with her collection of china which was almost totally destroyed.

I was told by a friend and fellow worker at a warehouse in Los Angeles about his childhood memory of an earthquake "It just wouldn't stop."

i

CHAPTER 1: WHAT IS A BIG QUAKE?

If someone talks about an explosion and fire, they could be talking about many different things. One type of explosion and fire could destroy a building or city, while another explosion and fire would be someone lighting a cigarette. Magnitude is the difference in very small and moderate or huge events. In this book I will be advising the reader about very big earthquakes. That is plural. Not The Big One but The Big Ones.

I have heard people in California say, "Earthquakes, I sleep through them." To sleep through a magnitude 7 or greater earthquake that has an epicenter within 20 miles of your bedroom would require you to be in a coma before it started. If the earthquake is 6 magnitude or more and within 10 miles of your location, you will wake up, and if you are in downtown Los Angeles, you will hear pictures falling off the wall and dogs barking and car alarms sounding. Any magnitude 5 or greater earthquake within 10 miles of the surface of the streets of a major, highly populated city, could be a killer quake.

The initial shaking could be a few seconds or minutes. When the shaking stops, it is followed by a temporary calm. The shaking then starts again. Death in the initial tremor is usually random, caused by falling power lines, or collapsing buildings, which might have been constructed with violations of the safety codes. Inadequate strength in bridges that were built many decades before codes were changed, might result in automobiles falling fifty feet into rivers or onto train tracks or freeways that are multilevel works of concrete art.

I lived in the Los Angeles area from 1956 until 1960. I lived in tall buildings that were hotel structures made of brick that dated back to very early in the twentieth century. I was living in the downtown area.

I lived in the very heart of a highly populated city with tall brick buildings all around me. The building in which I lived was 13 stories tall as were many buildings in Los Angeles. The height limit of thirteen stories was decided in those days to be the maximum for earthquake safety. The first building in Los Angeles that was built higher than 13 floors was the 26 story City Hall building. It has suffered earthquake damage.

Ask me how many earthquakes I felt between 1956 and 1960. The answer is, "None." The ground was very quiet in those days. It was building up stress. It was between quakes. The brick buildings were beautiful and they could withstand high winds and the January rains. Downtown L.A. was a pretty safe place to be. You could park your convertible on Broadway and go shopping for a half hour at Woolworth's or eat at Clifton's Cafeteria or even go to a movie at the Orpheum Theater and come back and find your car still there.

The ground probably moved a lot of times under my feet when I was walking and under the building in which I slept in those years between 1956 and 1960, but not more than a 4.5 magnitude of shaking. If the ground is shaking at 4.5 while you are walking down the street with the normal sound of traffic, it is likely you will not notice. You would notice a 4.5 if you were in an upper floor, or even a ground floor of a building and you were seated. You would not feel it if you were driving or riding on a bus or playing basketball in a school gym or working a physical job.

If a 4.5 quake occurred within 5 miles of my location while I was sleeping, it would probably wake me up. If it lasted only a couple of seconds, I would have thought it was probably a truck driving by or a plane flying overhead or a bad dream.

If you are seated in a single story residence and a quake of 4.5 magnitude occurs nearby, you will feel somewhat dizzy at first and then you will realize the room is moving a tiny bit. Imagine if the entire building is setting on a big trampoline and a car is driving around the edge of the trampoline. Several speed bumps are in the path of the moving car. As the car bounces over one, then another, slightly up and down, the trampoline bounces a very little bit, but everything on the trampoline, including your building and you, bounces very slowly up and down. No big deal, but you feel a slight movement. That is the sensation of being in a 4 or 4.5 quake. There could also be some noise, especially car alarms.

I moved from California in 1960 and I came back in 1980. I lived in the Hollywood area and later in the San Fernando Valley in Van Nuys. There had been a big quake while I was living out of the state.

On February 9, 1971, the Sylmar aka San Fernando Quake, killed 64 people. At least 2500 were injured. The quake was a 6.6 magnitude which is very big, but not The Big One. There were many aftershocks, of course. A hospital collapsed. Gas lines broke and started fires.

The first ground motion I felt was when I lived in Las Vegas in the 1960s. Atomic and Hydrogen bombs were tested at the Nevada Test Site, about 75 miles Northwest of the neon lights of The Strip. The news announcer on radio would mention something like, "It is seven AM and a test has just commenced. You should feel it in Las Vegas in thirty seconds." I would be sitting down so I could feel it. I always balanced a nickel on its edge on a coffee table to see if it would fall over. I had a microphone hanging over my piano for recording purposes. The mic hung from a rope that was attached to a metal eye hook in the ceiling. It normally just hung there and did not sway. I could see out my back window into my yard. A small tree grew about fifty feet back from the window.

The nickel never fell over. I could feel the dizzy sensation of the slight ground motion. It might have been a 3 or 3.5 magnitude, just enough to feel if you were expecting it. The mic did sway back and forth on the rope over the piano. As I looked out the back window I could see there was movement that looked like the tree was standing still and I was sitting still and the back window was sliding back and forth left to right. If I had been walking or driving I would not have noticed anything.

It is important for everyone who is facing a really big earthquake to know that there are thousands of earthquakes in the United States each year. If magnitude 1 and greater quakes are counted, there will be 10,000 and more each year in California. Alaska will have more. If magnitude 3 quakes and bigger are being counted, California will have about 200 per year. The ground wants to move an inch or so each year.

When I moved back to California in 1980 and stayed until 2006, I felt many quakes of 4.5 and greater. Some were very scary. The Northridge quake of 1994 killed 57 people and destroyed buildings and freeways. It was a 6.7 magnitude quake. It lasted from 7 to 15 seconds, depending on whether the count was eleven miles down or on the surface. There were many dozens of aftershocks, some greater than 5 magnitude. Gas lines broke and caused fires. Eleven hospitals were damaged. Underground parking in stucco buildings resulted in collapse and destruction of vehicles. Anything made of brick fell into pieces, including buildings, walls and chimneys.

The big quakes that I am focusing on in this book are those with magnitude 6.5 and greater. The killer quakes. I want to give some advice to those people who will not be moving to less populated areas. The areas most at risk in the US would include every city in California and the major cities in the Pacific Northwest and Memphis and St. Louis and their suburbs. All highly populated active zones.

If you can move comfortably to a less populated part of the country, you might avoid a big disaster.

CHAPTER 2: BEFORE THE BIG ONES

There are many things that can be done before the big quakes, that will save lives during and after the shaking. The destruction will be on a massive scale, but if you and your family are prepared you will be able to survive most of the things that will happen, depending on where you are.

Many times the big quakes happen at night. That is not a sure thing, but most people spend eight hours in bed each night. That gives you at least a 33% chance of being in bed when the shaking starts. The earthquake will be born full size. It does not start slowly and give you time to think of a plan. There will be a violent shaking, up and down, East, West, North or South and lots of noise. You will wake up. When you awaken and you know there is a big quake occurring, turn over into a crawling position immediately. It will not be easy. Practice that now, before the quake.

On your hands and knees you will be better able to crawl out of any rubble if your roof collapses or the ceiling comes loose. Do not lay on your back waiting for the shaking to stop. It will be very hard to crawl out of a pile of bricks or lumber on your back. Try to get into a crawling position at least once a week.

Before the quake, take down any mirrors or pictures hanging over your bed or anywhere that you might spend time. Do not have pictures and the china cabinet where they can pose a hazard to anyone seated on the sofa or at the kitchen table. Check ceiling fixtures for secure fit.

Tell the kids to remain in bed during any shaking and have everyone's shoes near the bed. You will probably be walking out of a room that is filled with broken glass from the windows. It is very possible your refrigerator door will open and glass jars and bottles will fall onto the floor. The refrigerator and Microwave will possibly fall over.

Check your refrigerator now to see if you can secure it to the wall with some wire and eye hooks before the quake. The door will still open and things will fall out but if the refrigerator is secure that will be one less threat. Start buying jelly and ketchup in plastic bottles now. Avoid glass.

Before there is a quake, I recommend having the natural gas turned off to your building. There are earthquake resistant meters that turn off the gas, but the gas line underground can break during a big quake. Read about the things that happened in the Sylmar and Northridge quakes and be serious about preventing the obvious dangers that exist. Condos and apartment buildings that have natural gas coming into the building could have big fire dangers when the ground begins to move.

Before the quake, take your dog on walks around the neighborhood. One day take the dog a couple of blocks South, next day go North. Familiarize your pet with the area a few hundred yards in every direction so that when the quake begins and the wall in the back yard comes down and the dog runs away, he or she will have an awareness of how to get back home when the shaking stops. Also invest in a tag that has the dog's name and your phone number and street address.

Before the earthquake meet your neighbors. Know the people in the next apartment or the family next door. You do not have to be annoying neighbors, but talk with them a bit about a plan for what to do to be helpful when there is a big quake. If you live in a high rise condo and you have elderly tenants on your floor, they will not have an elevator for several days. The elevator might be damaged beyond repair. Will you help someone who is not able to go shopping for food or water?

Make sure everyone in your family knows not to get into an elevator during or right after a big quake. The elevator will probably not fall to the ground, but it is very likely it will be stopped between floors.

Have some food and water and medical supplies on hand before they are needed. On the day or night of the initial shaking, remember the food in the freezer will be your first meals before canned food. The freezer probably will not have electricity, so get out the grill and cook whatever is likely to spoil in the first few days. Have a battery operated radio. Have a rope strong enough to lift an adult.

Contact a friend or relative who is out of town. Make sure everyone knows that person's phone number. If your phone works after the quake, contact that person and tell them where you are and if you are OK. If the kids are at school they should contact that person. Have a communication path that goes around the destroyed area.

If you are in the Pacific Northwest after the quake, plan to go to higher ground. There could be a tsunami coming in a minute or two. Do not drive onto a bridge or get into a subway car or run outside of a brick building when it is shaking.

Talk to the family and let them understand it is important to have some plans for the eventuality of a big quake. Be calm and practice some things before the shaking begins. You will be wise to buy a tent and some sleeping bags. You might not find any items on the shelf at stores after a big 7 magnitude or greater quake.

You might not have access to your vehicle if it is crushed in an underground parking area. If you do have a car available, gasoline might be in short supply. A bicycle purchased now could be some help, but it is likely you will be walking over rubble after the disaster. The shaking will continue every few minutes for the first week and then occasional big aftershocks will most likely make you dependent on some form of public conveyance, such as National Guard food and water delivery.

Have a plan for what you will do to help others. Have a plan with your neighbors in advance with an understanding about the need for security against looters. Do not become a problem yourself with any overreaction. Know how far you should go and when to back off. Talk it over with friends, family and neighbors in advance.

I will not tell you what is the best thing to do in various situations. Each neighborhood will be different. I can tell you that after the Big Ones in downtown Los Angeles there will be some people who will be more interested in digging out the rubble of the jewelry store or pawn shop, than saving the lives of your friends.

Prepare now for your mission after the initial shaking. If you are alive and well you will be a first responder. Have a shovel ready. When you get someone out let someone take them to a makeshift holding and treatment area. The National Guard and the Red Cross and other life saving agencies and government officials will quickly set up some sort of place to treat injured citizens.

Plan your own rationing in advance. You will want to eat the freezer food first. You will want to have drinking water that is protected in a safe place. If you are alone or with one other person or a big family, have a plan. That also is true if you are at school or at work or in a shopping center, decide now what you will do to survive and get back to your family or friends.

Kids especially should be aware that there will be frightened dogs running loose. Talk with your child's teachers, if possible, about a sensible plan for any eventuality. It is a good idea to check the school now.

Do not panic. It is very likely you will not be injured by the earthquake. You also can develop a plan that will help to calm others who otherwise might panic. Take charge whenever possible and help save as many lives as you can. That means you will plan now to have a few things that will increase your chance of being a survivor. Medical items and a battery radio and some duct tape and rope and ladders will be needed.

Also plan now for something you will want to have when you are dealing with a disaster. Have some money. Maybe a few silver eagle dollars for big things and just some change and a few dollars for necessary things that might be hard to get. Items like toilet paper or diapers or flashlights.

You will need a portable or chemical toilet or two. Most citizens will not be as prepared as you are. Life will become very primitive in the early days after the quake.

In the United States, FEMA will come in very quickly, even before the highways are cleared of debris. Have some identification papers for FEMA.. They actually did a very good job after the Northridge quake. They insisted on helping me and my neighbors even though we were doing fine. We had water and food but they offered more water and food. They offered cash for some people who had lost their apartment or condo. The Red Cross was also there quickly doing what it could.

Beware in advance of any "Earthquake Police" who show up trying to give orders. They might say "You can't go back inside your building." Meanwhile their associates are in that building looting whatever they can carry. You must demand to see any badges and identification of any would be officials. Educate your friends and neighbors in advance.

Talk with older people who went through moderate quakes to understand what to expect from a really big one. Meet with someone at your local hospital. Ask if they have a plan for The Big One and offer to help as a volunteer to assist if the hospital collapses, which has happened before. Hospitals can fall down when they are most needed.

A fire extinguisher should be in every home. In active zones it is a good idea to have a fire extinguisher in each room. Matches will be needed for outdoor cooking and heating. A magnifying glass can be helpful for starting a fire if there are no matches available.

Earthquake insurance is OK if your insurance company is stable and not likely to go bankrupt after the claims roll in. Depending on your situation, an earthquake insurance policy can help replace physical things. Check the rates and the deductible amounts of different policies. Will your car insurance pay for earthquake damage?

If you live near an ocean or big river, invest in a rubber inflatable raft. A small boat or even an inner tube that can keep you afloat during a tsunami or changes in the height of a river.

Have one or more solar power panels to charge cell phones.

CHAPTER 3: DURING THE BIG ONES

The Big One or Ones begin. Too late to move. You are somewhere and something big happens. The earth begins to shake violently for several minutes. Maybe just one or two minutes. Maybe for five minutes. You are wherever you happen to be at that time of day. When the earth stops shaking it seems calm for a few seconds. Then it starts shaking again. Then it stops again. Maybe for a minute or two. It will shake every few minutes for the next twenty four hours. Some of the ground motion during aftershocks might be over 5 magnitude, which is big enough to do more damage. If the first quake was a 7 or greater strength, it is likely you will feel a 6 magnitude event before 48 hours has passed. You will probably feel at least one more 7 magnitude aftershock or new quake before one year has passed.

During that initial shake you will hear loud sounds. Things will be falling and breaking. Some people will scream. Dogs will bark and car alarms will go off. Electrical transformers will, in some cases, fall off their poles. Some transformers will sputter with a sound that I would describe as a phht. That is not a misspelling. It begins with an "F" sound that is drawn out for a couple of seconds and then a "pop" that is like a bursting balloon.

You will feel some movements in different directions. Up and down and a bit of a sense of motion to the left or right or North or South. Some houses in California, especially, will slide down hillsides. That does happen. The ground under you is probably trying to move North or South or East or West as much as five or ten feet. You and your house and a thimble or a mountain will all move five or ten feet with it. You might go outside after the quake and you will notice the house across the street that used to be directly across from you is now offset to the left or right.

If you are at home and in your bed when the big shaking begins, try to turn over onto your tummy so you will be in a position to crawl out of the rubble. Nobody wants to crawl out of the rubble, but some people will have to do just that. If it is you, be in a good crawling position.

If you are at work or at school, do what the advance plan for earthquakes has taught you. Do not panic. It is OK to be frightened. Just remain as calm as possible and you can tell those around you everything will be OK when the shaking stops. Tell everyone the shaking will be stopping very soon and you will all go outside to see who needs assistance.

If you are driving, you will feel the big quake that is happening. Slow down and pull to the right if possible, as if you were being followed by an emergency vehicle with red or blue lights flashing. Remember the people who are driving near your vehicle, who are probably bad drivers on good days, have never experienced a big earthquake. Do not step out of your vehicle if cars are driving by. Try to find a safe place to park away from brick buildings.

Do not drive onto a bridge if you can avoid it. If you are on a bridge try to drive forward at a moderate speed while you watch for any buckling of the roadway. If there is a hole where the road surface of the bridge has fallen, stop your car and leave the flashing signals turned on to warn others. When it appears safe, get out of your car and try to get to a safe section of the bridge walkway where pedestrian traffic will be safer.

During the motion, plan your steps when the ground becomes still again. If you are in a single family home, plan to gather outside in the yard away from chimneys. There will be a lot of shaking during the first hour. You will most likely survive the first ground motion. Your house is probably very sturdy and built according to codes.

If you are trapped inside your house try to crawl to a door or window. If you exit a window be sure to place a blanket or several blankets over the frame that has broken glass so you can get out without cutting your hands and other parts of your body. If you cannot move you will have to wait for rescue while you call out to anyone outside. They are looking for you already.

If you are trapped and cannot move, conserve your energy as much as possible. Rescue operations start immediately with neighbors and friends pulling stones and bricks off the pile of rubble that once was your house.

You also should try to dig your way out slowly and safely. Be careful. You probably will be moving around in the dark. Get any stick or two by four to use as a digging tool. Figure which direction is up and head in that direction. Say something occasionally to let those who are searching for you know where you are.

When the first shaking stops, if you are not injured, you are a first responder. See if there are injuries to your family, friends or neighbors.

Most of what happens to people in a big quake is similar to what happens in a tornado or flood or forest fire. Homes are destroyed and people are injured and some lose their lives. The big differences with earthquakes is they do not stop. The next hour or day could bring a huge aftershock that stops rescue efforts. Freeways that are damaged but standing might be brought down by an aftershock.

A really big earthquake can cover a huge area. It can trigger movement in nearby faults. If the San Andreas fault rips open in Southern California, it might put pressure on the Hayward fault or vice versa. High rise newer construction could result in swaying upper floors that have accelerated movement of office furniture and file cabinets. The glass might withstand the pressure of a file cabinet falling against it, or it might break with some furniture heading for the street below. Don't stand under any office buildings, especially old brick buildings. Do not walk under overhead telephone or electric wires connected to the swaying telephone poles.

It is best to gather your family as close to your home as possible and begin to help other people who have injuries or find people who are missing. Remain organized and expect to see a FEMA tent appear within 48 hours. If the big quake you just felt was a foreshock, there could be a bigger movement coming within a few days. Check your house. If it is sturdy, you probably can sleep there. The faucet water will be dark if it runs at all and it will not be safe to drink. It probably will be too dirty to use even for washing for the first week after the initial shake.

The "during" phase of an earthquake or series of earthquakes goes on for weeks or months or longer. You will be repairing and filling out forms and helping neighbors for a long time. Your supply of canned foods and bottled water will eventually run out. The National Guard will be doing all they can to bring in needed blankets, food and water. So will the Red Cross and private agencies. You will get electricity restored before the water is clear. It is likely the phones will work right away but you might find it a long wait for a dial tone.

Try to get a community established in your area. Encourage a reconstruction effort. Help calm the kids by giving them small jobs to do to let them feel they are helping. Depending on their ages you can have them sing songs for the rescue workers or help pick up some small objects after the glass is cleared away. Have good conversations with your kids and others. Kids and dogs might be able to hear or see things in collapsed structures that adults might not see or hear. Be sure to not let kids wander into any structures or get too far away from your observation.

The main goal is to get everything back to normal and even better as quickly as possible. You will notice something during the ground motion that occurs which will help you understand where the ground is going. It is not just shaking, it is heading in a direction.

If you have a wall in your backyard that falls over, it might fall to the North. Then you go inside your house and notice that the tall cabinet fell to the North. The lamp that was on a table fell to the North. If that is what happened, the land is probably shifting to the South. How does it help to know that?

Imagine a long bus sitting on a city street. If twenty strong men pushed real hard on one side of the bus, they could get it rocking and turn it over. If those same twenty strong men pushed on the front of the bus it would not turn over.

If you have a table in your kitchen and you place a tall cereal box, like corn flakes, on the table, with the front of the box facing you as you stand to the South of the table, and you push the table one time very hard to the North, the cereal box will fall face down to the South. If you push the table just as hard from the West to the East, the cereal box will not fall.

Waves travel from the epicenter of the quake. If you are West of the epicenter most waves will be coming from the East. That will not always be exactly the case, but usually you will notice a pattern of falling objects falling to the East or North or a particular direction. You will be able to look at previous damage and tell what is going to go next.

If you live in a mobile home park, some long trailers that face in one direction will suffer very little damage while trailers that appear to be the same size and style, but face in a different direction, will suffer great damage. This is the kind of thing kids might catch on to before adults. Talk with the young and the old and ask what they have noticed that they have not mentioned. It could help you decide where to place that tall cabinet when you are dealing with aftershocks.

During the early aftershocks, before the electricity and water have been restored, it could be necessary to drain the water from the hot water heater. Let that be done by someone who knows how to do it. Strain the water through a clean white towel or washcloth or some clean, non dyed fabric. and if possible, boil it and let it cool before drinking it.

CHAPTER 4: AFTER THE BIG ONES

After the quake might mean immediately after the first tremor has stopped or after the last aftershock has stopped. All of these things can be helpful to make the world of normal living return. The first good news after a quake is that a lot of stress has been released. That first shock might be the biggest. You will definitely feel many aftershocks. You made it through the biggest one and you are now a veteran. Remind your friends and family constantly that the worst is probably behind you and your immediate responsibility is to save the lives of trapped victims. You also have to protect each other in the days ahead with a community approach to survival if you live in a highly populated downtown area.

If you are in a suburban area, you will have less rubble than those who live downtown. Hopefully your family will be together or safe in separate locations. If your child is walking home from a school, advise them to walk in a group carrying some sticks or baseball bats to scare off any stray dogs. Do not try hitting the dogs. Just waving the big sticks should do the job. Having an adult leading them is better.

Cooking can be done in a fire pit if it is not too windy. Baked potatoes in aluminum foil are easy to cook and the food in the freezer or refrigerator will spoil before the electricity returns to normal. Eventually the food will run out, especially for seniors in a hospital or condo type building. It is likely FEMA and the Red Cross will arrive within a couple of days with some food and blankets and water. You should rely on yourself until there is a big government presence. The National Guard will establish some form of security. Beware of how you deal with any looters. If possible detain them somehow by making a citizen's arrest. Do not try to tackle several armed thugs. Use your common sense when trouble appears.

I would suggest not straying far during the first weeks after the big ones. There will be plenty to do close to your residence. If you happen to be a visitor from another area who just happened to be caught in the earthquake, feel free to go back home, if possible. There might not be any flights and roads might be closed for a month or longer. Just help in whatever way you can and contact someone back home and let them know the situation. Everyone caught in the middle of a disaster is part of the first responders or part of the clean up detail. Some people will be suffering broken bones and will be needing aid. It is a time to pitch in and plan for the good times to come.

Video cameras and phone cameras should be used to document what is happening and what each person is learning from the situation. You will be training future generations of earthquake victims.

During the aftershocks have the cameras collecting the images and sounds. Videos are best when the panning and zooming are not used at the same time. Pan slowly and then zoom slowly. Describe what is happening.

For earthquakes you will be best off to be on the ground away from buildings. For tsunamis you will be safest atop a tall hill or on the upper floors of a strong building. Even after a year you will want to be on guard for where to go quickly when a big tremor starts.

You will begin to rebuild on your same lot or in a new place. Some small mobile home communities will appear. There will still be tents on lawns after a year has passed. People will go back to work and some areas will become schools where kids begin to study again. Broken bones will mend. People will buy cars and drive on new construction as freeways and bridges return to a new normal.

How you react before, during and after the quake will determine what happens for you and those around you from now on. Some people will show heroism immediately after the first ground motion. Some will do great things later. Some will be trapped for many hours or days and crawl out alive and survive what nature threw at them.

You will see piles of rubble containing refrigerators and microwaves and TVs. You will be protecting important papers and pictures and favorite toys. The family car might be gone, but the kid's bicycle made it. You will have new keepsakes. Life will change but you can rebuild your own space. The high rise buildings might need extensive repairs or some will be torn down. Jobs will disappear and other jobs will become available, especially in construction.

Plan before, survive during and recover after.

When a year or two has passed and the ground is stable, your area probably will be quiet for many years. The buildings that will be constructed after the big shake will be strong enough to withstand the next one, we hope.

CHAPTER 5: BIGGEST EARTHQUAKES

The 1960 Valdivia earthquake in Chile has been estimated to have had a magnitude of approximately 9.5. That means it is the largest earthquake ever measured. There have probably been quakes as large and larger during past centuries but they had no way to measure the strength until modern times. Most quakes that occured before the Twentieth Century are measured by educated guesses. The Valdivia quake was not under a major city.

There were tsunamis. Not just one, but several. The quake lasted about ten minutes. Between 1,000 and 6,000 people were killed in Valdivia. Other people died in Hilo, Hawaii, thousands of miles away. A huge tsunami came ashore as a surprise to the Hawaiian citizens. The wave was more than 30 feet high. Along the coast of Chile the wave was estimated to be over 80 feet high.

The second largest quake ever recorded was the Alaska Good Friday Earthquake of 1964. It was measured at 9.2 magnitude. It also was accompanied by tsunamis that killed people not only in Alaska, but also in California, where 13 people died from the tsunami and in Oregon 5 people were killed. The total death toll was 139. The largest tsunami wave from the 1964 Alaska quake was recorded in Shoup Bay, Alaska, with a height of over 220 ft Most casualties in the quake were related to the tsunamis, not ground motion.

The 2004 Indian Ocean Earthquake was the third largest recorded earthquake in history. It killed about 250,000 people in 14 countries. Most of the deaths were attributed to the tsunamis. Coastal cities are always in more danger of having deadly destruction during ground motion not only from falling buildings and objects, but the deadly huge waves that come onshore with walls of water sometimes over 100 feet in height. The quake was measured at 9.2. The magnitude of quakes includes not only how violent the shaking might be, but also how large an area is affected and how long the motion lasts. There were, of course, many aftershocks from that quake.

Fourth largest earthquake ever measured with modern equipment was the 2011 earthquake off the Pacific Coast of Tohoku, Japan. It was measured at 9.1 and caused the deaths of almost 16,000 people. A tsunami with waves up to 133 feet in height caused damage not only to buildings and roads and railway systems, but it triggered a dangerous nuclear incident that could have proven to be a more deadly hazard than the ground motion and tsunamis combined.

The 1952 Severo-Kurilsk tsunami was the fifth greatest earthquake recorded. It was not a land quake. It occurred in the ocean about 80 miles from Kamchatka. The magnitude 9 earthquake caused three tsunamis with waves about 50 feet in height to come ashore in Severo-Kurilsk. Most of the citizens ran to higher ground after the quake. They escaped the first wave, but made the mistake of returning to their homes after the water receded. The second wave killed over 2300 of the 6000 residents. The third wave was not as big and did not do much more damage to the town which was mostly destroyed. The survivors were taken to Russia and resettled.

The 1950 Assam-Tibet earthquake was measured at 8.6. It killed between 1500 and 3500 people It is the largest measured quake that was not in or near the ocean. It was caused by continental plate movement. There was no tsunami associated with this quake, however people drowned in swollen rivers that had changed their course during the shaking.

The 1965 Rat Islands earthquake was the seventh largest measured quake with a magnitude of 8.7. It did cause a tsunami with waves of about 40 feet height. Despite the size of the quake and the tsunami that was generated, very little damage occurred and there was no loss of life.

In 1957 the eighth largest measured earthquake occurred near the Andreanof Islands. The magnitude was 8.6. There was no loss of life and about 5 million dollars in damage. Even though the quake was near Alaska, it caused a tsunami that resulted in a fifty foot high wave that hit Hawaii. A warning was issued early enough to cause people to leave the beaches where the wave hit.

The 2005 Nias-Simeulue quake occurred off the West coast of Northern Sumatra, Indonesia. It was rated as 8.6 magnitude. About 915 people were killed by the shaking, but the tsunami was small for such a large tremor and damage was limited.

The 2012 Indian Earthquakes with magnitude of 8.6 and 8.2 were huge quakes, but whether a large tsunami occurred is still uncertain. The two quakes just hours apart were centered near the Indian Province of Aceh. Warnings were immediately issued and the people moved quickly to higher ground. Fewer than ten people died as a result of the quake and none from tsunamis. The deaths were caused by heart attacks which were most likely the result of the heavy ground shaking. The quake was unusual in that some places near the epicenter had less shaking than places farther away.

Those ten quakes were the largest recorded so far with modern technology. The major killer in most of those quakes was from tsunamis. There are, of course, other threats to human life during a quake. Fire is something that happens when a big city is hit directly. If there is a gas line or an open flame somewhere in the city it can take many lives and destroy a lot of property. Hospital patients are at risk if there is a prolonged power outage. A person who cannot run to higher ground or walk down a flight of stairs is in greater danger than healthy active young people. As much as the ground shaking is frightening, it is what comes after the shaking has stopped that can be most deadly. Also remember what comes after a very big quake is a very big aftershock.

The biggest recorded quakes happened in recent years, historically. There were some great quakes in the past millions of years which have changed the appearance of mountains and valleys and coastlines and rivers. Some past quakes which have happened before modern measuring equipment was invented, have been studied and in many cases there are written records of what damage they caused.

On January 23, 1556, in Shensi, China, an earthquake occurred which took more than 830,000 lives. The magnitude is unknown. Most of the buildings in the city, perhaps all the buildings collapsed. Fissures split the ground open. Water came to the surface causing liquefaction.

In Tangshan, China, on July 27, 1976, there was an earthquake which was not as high in magnitude as some of the "big" quakes. The magnitude was 7.5. The death toll was officially stated as 250,000 but some estimates place the number of people killed by the tremor at 655,000.

In Haiti on January 12, 2010, a magnitude 7.0 quake took more than 200,000 lives. Much of the disaster was blamed on poor construction of buildings and difficulty for rescue teams to reach victims in the rubble. Haiti is a poor country and it does not have the vehicles and hospitals which are necessary for quick reaction to save lives.

Damghan, Iran, had a big earthquake on December 22, 856. The magnitude is unknown. The death toll was over 200,000 people. History tells us much about the earthquakes that devastated some areas, but there were no video cameras or devices to measure magnitude in those days.

Haiyuan, Ningxia, China on December 16, 1920, saw a magnitude 7.8 quake which caused massive landslides. Open fissures occurred during the shaking. Sujiahe, a city, was completely buried in a few seconds. The estimated death toll was over 200,000.

Ardabil, Iran, was hit with Iran's second very deadly earthquake in the 9th Century. It struck on March 23, 893. The death toll from the quake is estimated at 150,000. These quakes happened when houses were made with no special code considerations. If this same quake occurred today, the death toll would almost certainly be much less.

There are several messages screaming from the historical accounts of death, injury and destruction from previous earthquakes. One lesson to be learned is that after a gigantic quake there could be a tsunami. After a big quake there will be aftershocks. After a big shaker there will be a need to quickly rescue your neighbors.

Before a big ground motion occurs, make your residence as safe as possible. Don't let things fall on you. Take action now. If you can move to a less populated location, that will be safer. A single family home is safer than a big old brick hotel or a stucco apartment building. If something needs repair and reinforcement and you can get it done, do it.

Have a plan for each family member where they live, where they work and where they go to school. Prepare for before, during and after. Do not be a casualty if you can do something now to prevent it.

Remember the stories of earthquake tolls on life and property. Big storms and fires can kill many people, but earthquakes can kill more. Some earthquakes took almost one million lives. Some earthquakes are accompanied by fires or volcanoes or tsunamis. Earthquakes are followed by more earthquakes.

Today's realities can cause the death toll to be higher if large scale gang activity occurs in an environment that is not protected by local law enforcement. You will be required to put out fires if fire engines are not able to reach your area due to damaged streets.

My purpose in writing this book is to save a few lives by helping the readers focus on what is a very real threat. The shaking probably will not kill you or even hurt you. Be prepared.

The biggest measured earthquake is yet to come.

CHAPTER 6: WHO WILL HELP?

The government will be trying to help you and all the survivors of any big quake in the US. That is probably true in most countries. There are specific departments of the US federal government that will act quickly.

When the Northridge quake occurred in 1994, FEMA moved in the next day with tents and some supplies like blankets and water, and many people who were helping homeowners fill out forms for aid. FEMA is the Federal Emergency Management Agency. They actually gave money to people to help them get repair work done for houses and apartments and car damage. They were very helpful for many families.

The National Guard and Army Reserve will be quickly mobilized. They will try to restore a sense of law and order. They also will try to cope with fires that might be raging. Some agencies such as the Red Cross will arrive with some help. Churches and hospitals will do what they can to provide assistance. Hospitals, especially, will need volunteers.

You will also help yourself and others. You will encourage your healthy neighbors to spend some of their time helping injured people. There will be much to do. Doctors and babysitters will be in short supply. Security guards will be on edge.

The police department will try to respond but they will not be as fast as they are when there is no emergency. Emergency status will be declared by federal level authorities. That will increase the speed of aid getting to where it is most needed.

You and your neighbors will try to offer first aid and you will try to dig out victims whose houses have collapsed. Your routine will change instantly. You will recognize the real needs around you. You will volunteer to help all the first responders.

Now, let's mention something that sounds impossible in the United States. There is an executive order that dates back to the Kennedy Presidency which has been the subject of much controversy. Check the internet and search for FEMA Executive Order. Also check National Defense Resources Preparedness. This is something you can see in print but which the federal government denies ever will happen.

The basic idea of the original executive order and the additions to that order by many other presidents over the years is to confiscate or take charge of all areas of public needs during any National Emergency. Supposedly the president would declare the emergency and take over all broadcast facilities and sources of water and food in any given place or time. If you had stored some water and somebody down the street did not have water, the National Guard or some powerful arm of the government would take your water or food or blankets and distribute them. Is that a good idea? Who makes the decision? Will you be searched? Remember there is no shortage of denials that such an order would ever be contemplated, but it does exist and you can search and read what authority the government claims to have. My guess is it will not happen on a wide scale, anywhere. Other nations have other rules that could be implemented.

I believe for most people sharing resources will occur with neighbors and strangers. If rescue organizations and government departments act quickly many lives will be saved.

The good news I will note here is that after a huge earthquake and maybe a year of aftershocks, the ground will settle down, perhaps for many decades. The first ten minutes will be the scariest part of a big earthquake. After that people will start to focus on saving lives and recovering from the losses. You will see heroes whom you never noticed before it got so crazy. You might be one of those heroes.

Outside help will come. Water and food will arrive. Law and order will gradually be restored. Churches might become temporary hospitals. The people with gasoline generators will be providing light for nighttime digging. Use the small solar generators for recharging phones.

Whatever the situation, make it better. Everyone can do something that will be helpful. The United States is not the only place in the world expecting very big earthquakes. Wherever you live, be ready to help your family and friends and neighbors. The US is probably best prepared for such emergencies, but wherever you are after a big quake, your first helping hand will be from a local source.

CHAPTER 7: GOLD OR SILVER?

Many people will have some gold or silver or cash hidden away somewhere for the emergency. If you have such a treasure, or diamonds and jewelry and other valuables, is that a good idea? You will hear ads on the radio or TV telling you to have five percent of your wealth in gold or silver. Think about what the situation will be. If you are in a condo or apartment or hotel in a big city are you going to go walking down the stairs and into the street holding a gold bar? Will you show a few silver dollars to a crowd of people and ask them to give you some food or water? After showing some valuables will you go back into the building to sleep?

This is a chapter I do not like to write, but the reality of a post earthquake environment requires you, the survivor, to think honestly. In downtown Los Angeles and probably in many other areas, there are lots of jewelry stores and pawn shops. If they crumble, will some individuals try to beat the system by digging for gold instead of survivors?

I have watched many earthquake documentaries and there always seems to be a scene of a meter that is tracing a jagged line on a graph. If that is all you or I have to worry about during an earthquake, a needle moving, there is no problem. The problems will be getting friends and neighbors and strangers out of collapsed structures. Store shelves will quickly become emptied of supplies. There you are.

Gold is worth something and might be good for someone who wants to buy a car or a house or something big. You will not want to give a gold bar to someone for a peanut butter sandwich. A silver eagle is a better form of payment for a few days supply of food if someone is selling canned food or sandwiches. The real answer is to have some food stored away. It can save your life and the lives of your family members.

I want this book to be real and helpful. I am not going to tell you that everyone is good and will be pitching in. Most people will be helping each other. I saw that happen at a trailer park where I lived in Van Nuys in 1994, just a few miles from the epicenter of the Northridge quake. Every space was checked within one hour of the first massive ground motion. Everyone was accounted for by the next day. People set up tents in their small yards and some slept outside for the first few nights. There was no need for gold or silver then. The roads in the area were drivable. I did not experience any price gouging or problems with access to health services or food. FEMA sent a representative to check to see if anyone needed emergency treatment. I did my normal routine shopping. There were no looters in our park. We did set up a volunteer guard team. Our gated community did not suffer a great deal of damage, although one section of our cement brick wall collapsed. We were lucky. If someone had gold or silver stored away in their mobile home, I never knew about it. Keep in mind it was not a huge 7.5 or greater quake and it did not devastate our area. There was nobody who needed to be dug out.

Every city will have its own problems after a gigantic quake. Saint Louis and Memphis could suffer huge losses of life if an 8 magnitude quake hits the New Madrid Fault again. Maybe gold or silver will be something you will want to have tucked away for the emergency. I will not have gold stored anywhere for bad times. I will try to have more food and medical supplies than I will likely need. I will definitely try to help some others but I would help my family and friends first. Silver eagle coins are impressive and they have a value much lower than gold bars, so they could be used to trade for food for a group of people. If you have a wheelbarrow filled with gold bars or gold coins, where and when do you sleep?

You will be best off to organize some of your neighbors into a unit that is going to survive first, then thrive. Have security for food and medicine but try to share with those who need help most.

There are many things that will be more valuable than gold after a massive quake. A shovel, a good dog who can help rescue efforts, a hammer and nails, a ladder and a solar phone charger, for example. You probably will be on your own for the first 24 hours and you will have limited assistance for 72 hours. Depending on your location you could have looting and/or gang problems after a few days.

I will not suggest any protective responses because that will be best determined by you and those around you. Hopefully the cool heads will prevail and give consideration to each situation as things develop. Several US major cities will someday have a huge earthquake. Seattle will have problems different from Memphis or Los Angeles or San Francisco. You will face a unique situation. Roads, buildings, bridges, subway systems and people will suffer different stresses that could need quick recoveries.

CHAPTER 8: VOLCANOES

Some states in the US have active volcanoes. Other states have dormant volcanoes which could become active again. Sometimes a big earthquake begins because of volcanic activity. "It can't happen here." Maybe it can. Maybe it will. You have heard of Mount Saint Helens and Yellowstone and you probably have heard of Mount Rainier and Mount Shasta. There are others. Hawaii is an island created by a series of volcanic eruptions over thousands of years. Alaska has more than 50 active volcanoes.

There is a volcano in Mississippi that erupted 65 million years ago. You probably would feel safe peeking into the top of that one, but I would stay back. There are people who travel the world looking for volcanoes to study. There is a viral video that shows a big volcano erupting with the geologist/volcanologist being too close and being killed by the pyroclastic flow. Do not go near a volcano that is active. If I lived near Mount Shasta or Mount Rainier or Mount Saint Helens, I would move.

My logic is based on factual studies of how people die doing what they do well. Airline pilots are the most likely people to die in plane crashes. Sky divers are most likely to die falling from an airplane. Elephant trainers are most likely to... you get the picture. A volcanologist is in danger of dying from being too close to a volcano.

A volcano has all the dangers associated with earthquakes, plus fire and pyroclastic flow. Study the possibility of an eruption at Mount Shasta or Mount Rainier. It is real. It could destroy some towns and cover some highways with lava. The 5 freeway could be buried in a big eruption. The ash that falls from a distant volcano erupting could cause breathing problems, or fires or deaths many miles away. Lava and pyroclastic flow do not stop at walls or fences.

Some natural disasters could be worse than an earthquake caused by a volcanic eruption. If a meteor the size of Manhattan Island or the size of the Moon were to hit planet Earth head on, it could destroy every living animal on Earth. It could possibly snuff out plant life and leave nothing but some big rocks going around in big circles.

Of the natural disasters which are likely to happen sometime soon, the worst would be a combination of earthquakes, volcanic eruption and tsunamis near highly populated areas. That could happen in the US, and it certainly has occurred in various parts of the world. We have heard the ancient story of Pompeii and Mount Vesuvius. The eruption in 79 AD killed thousands of people in several nearby cities. Today, three million people are near enough to Mount Vesuvius to become victims of its next huge explosion. If it erupts with the power of previous recorded explosions, the power released would be many thousands of times greater than the atomic bomb blasts at Hiroshima and Nagasaki.

A volcano in California or Oregon or Washington could at some time cause a blast that would be felt as an earthquake, but the ash fallout could kill crops in states hundreds or thousands of miles away. The greater the population in the area nearby, the greater the possibility of loss of life.

As bad as a volcanic eruption might seem, it could be far worse if a supervolcano explodes. The Yellowstone supervolcano last had a major eruption 640,000 years ago. It might not happen for another million years. There are some other supervolcanoes in places like Iceland, New Zealand, Japan, Russia and even in Idaho. Search Snake River Plains Volcano.

Some scientists believe there is a connectivity way down below to chambers that might hold magma and have several surface outlets. Yellowstone has many peaks which could be considered active but not in danger of erupting on a massive scale anytime soon.

The worst natural disaster that is likely sometime on Earth, without any outside help from orbiting bodies, is a supervolano eruption even in a remote area. The ash cloud could cover continents far away from the site of the eruption. If humans survived it, they probably would live underground for several years after the eruption, if not longer. There are people living in underground cities now in several places around the world. The cities were originally built to survive nuclear war.

The good news about volcanoes is there are no supervolcanoes expected to erupt soon. There should be a few years warning before it happens. Some private companies now are planning commercial space travel for tourists who want to go to the moon and beyond. For now it would be considered a round trip, but maybe some pioneers will want to move to places not of this world.

CHAPTER 9: STORMS VS. EARTHQUAKES

In California you will often hear people giving the excuse for not moving away from the coming Big Ones. Some people will say "If I move to the Midwest to avoid an earthquake, I will be trading earthquakes for tornadoes. Both places are dangerous." That is true to some extent. If we talk about a small or medium sized earthquake or even a large earthquake of 6.5 magnitude, it probably won't kill more people or do more damage than an F4 tornado. An F5 tornado would be even worse. Why move?

The reason for moving is the overall destruction that will occur if a magnitude 7 or 7.5 or even greater earthquake occurs under a big, highly populated area, the damage and death toll will be far worse than an F5 tornado. The tornado, even the biggest tornado, might be two miles wide and it could stay on the ground for several hours and do damage to a path that is twenty or even fifty miles long. Fifty times two equals 100 square miles of damage. If it hits you it does as much damage as any disaster. But... it will not come back tomorrow and spawn smaller tornadoes for the next year and then smack you with the same force one year later.

A big tornado is not a continuing event like an earthquake. The ground will shake for many months to come. Some aftershocks will be moderate, maybe 5 magnitude. Others will be at 6 and even a couple of big aftershocks near the strength of the initial shaking will be expected. The damage in Southern California will cover at least one thousand square miles. Tall buildings will fall. Shopping centers will have collapsed roofs. Schools and hospitals will be destroyed. Things will fall on people. With a storm, there will be a warning. With an earthquake it is come as you are. If you are in bed you will have to quickly change position because the ceiling might fall on you. Really.

Rescue aid coming in your direction will have to find detours around damaged airports, damaged shipping docks, damaged railways and collapsed tunnels and freeways that are missing big sections of concrete. Your place of employment might be gone. All of the plumbing fixtures in your house or condo will be broken to bits. Water coming into the city will be undrinkable for awhile. The small and moderate earthquakes are not likely to cause anything other than a few broken bottles falling out of the refrigerator. A big tornado is scary and can do much more damage than a small quake does. The comparison of a tornado to an earthquake usually shows the damage from a big storm versus the most recent 5 magnitude or smaller quake.

What I am describing in this book is a huge earthquake. We have not had one in the United States under a big city since 1906. We are not "due" because there is no way of knowing when an earthquake of great magnitude will occur. The USGS suggests there is a one percent chance of a big earthquake each month in Southern California. They do not give any odds for a huge 7.5 or larger ground motion. They cannot guess with any accuracy. They do try. They know it is coming.

A weather forecaster can say with some reliability 24 hours in advance of a tornado that a certain area is likely to experience tornado cells and the residents hear the warning sirens. So far that cannot be done with quakes. Probably within ten years there will be a warning system. A half minute warning could be given to Los Angeles residents if an 8 magnitude quake occurred on the San Andreas fault. The way that would happen is if the ground began to shake at a high rate of motion, a radio signal could be sent to Los Angeles to operate a special siren. The radio signal would reach Los Angeles before the ground motion. That is actually being worked on and it could be designed and built at low cost. It would save many lives of people in offices and schools and shopping centers who could move away from big glass windows and seek shelter under some table or desk. Think of how a few seconds warning could help window washers in high rise buildings and mechanics working under automobiles and someone standing on a high ladder or cutting branches in a tall tree.

A storm can bring lightning damage. It can bring local flooding and also cause flooding downstream. A huge earthquake can and will bring down power lines. In the 1994 Northridge quake, the only person in Van Nuys who died as a quake fatality was someone who was hit by a falling electrical wire. The flooding from a huge quake can be seen by looking at YouTube or other internet videos of tsunami damage.

Remember, a huge earthquake under a major city anywhere will likely result in massive casualties. If the buildings and highways are incredibly well built, the number of survivors will be near 100%. What happens after the shaking is still a mystery.

CHAPTER 10: REVIEW

A big earthquake will come to a city near you if you live in an active area. In the US, the active areas which will definitely someday have a huge ground motion include Southern California, Central California, Northern California, Hawaii, Alaska, Memphis and Saint Louis. Each of these areas can have a magnitude 7.5 and greater. Some locations can expect a magnitude 8 or 9 or greater ground motion. There also will be big earthquakes under major cities on every continent. Not at the same time.

Each of these places has had a major quake in the past. There is no "due date." Nobody and no agency can say when it will happen. The USGS can give a percentage of a chance you might experience a 6 or greater quake during the beginning of any month. They are guessing the odds. Sometimes when they notice unusual activity with a swarm of moderate quakes, they will increase their guess of what the odds are for something occurring that month. They cannot say if it will be daytime or night or workday or weekend.

After the huge quake they will predict many aftershocks, but again, not when. Badly built buildings will fall down. Get into a crawling position when you first feel a major tremor. You will not be able to walk or run during the shaking without falling down. Stay away from anything made of brick, including walls and chimneys and buildings. If you are inside a brick building do not run outside while it is shaking. Bricks will be falling. Chances are the building will remain upright if it has a steel frame. All the plumbing and electricity and elevators will not be usable until repair crews get to it, and maybe the building will never be repaired. It might be in need of being torn down.

Expect fires and floods, depending on where you are. I do not think a tsunami will accompany a Los Angeles earthquake, but it could. I would expect a tsunami to hit Southern California if there is a big quake in the Pacific Northwest. A Southern California quake on the San Andreas fault could cause major damage to Las Vegas hotels.

Your thoughts will be about survival at first, then rescuing others, then organizing your friends, family and neighbors into a group that can best deal with anything that is going on. There could be fires and floods to deal with.

As I have mentioned before, the food in the freezer and refrigerator might begin to spoil if the electricity is off for a long time, so eat that first. Water is in every hot water heater that did not become damaged. Hopefully you will have enough first aid supplies for any early injuries. If you have a generator, use it wisely. Lights for nighttime rescue digging might be the main way to utilize a gasoline operated generator. If you have enough flashlights or car headlamps to make a rescue site visible for workers, the generator might supply power for digging tools.

In highly populated areas there could be massive casualties after a magnitude 7.5 quake. It could bring out the best in people and it could bring out the criminal element of looters and gang members. Survival and security will be something to plan for if necessary. I will not encourage anyone to take the law into their own hands. Hopefully all will go smoothly and government agencies will be able to get to the hardest hit areas quickly You will be wise to always sleep near your clothes and shoes and credit cards and cash. Have at least one fire extinguisher nearby. A crowbar or tire iron might be helpful to make doors open after the door jamb is broken during the shaking. .

Inside your car you will need some bottles of water and first aid supplies. You might be driving when the first big one hits. You would be wise to have a few snacks in the car, maybe in the glove compartment or trunk. If your car is big enough for a folding bicycle or skateboard of some sort, it could give you some means of transportation while major roads are damaged or jammed.

Remember, someone is looking for you and thinking of you. There really are some federal agencies that will try to provide help and relief and medical and economic assistance. The aid workers begin to arrive within a few hours and they will have tents and clerical personnel filling out forms within a couple of days. The National Guard and Army Reserve units will make an appearance within a few days. Volunteer medical teams will be in most of the major areas that have collapsed buildings. Some of those buildings will be hospitals and schools and malls. You will need lots of trained people and dogs working in ruins of what were big buildings last week. You will probably be spending much of your day volunteering alongside your neighbors. If you are in a downtown area where there were thousands of people in each square mile, you will very likely be eating your meals at some community gathering spot. You might be eating in a corner of your condo or apartment building or hotel room. You were fortunate. You planned ahead. You survived.

You now begin to plan for a quiet, non shaking future after the aftershocks have stopped. It might be another year with plenty of shaking, but it will gradually come to rest again. Maybe by the time the great big earthquake happens science will have a way to make it a gentle trampoline experience. Someday the quakes will be predicted like weather is now forecast.

No mirrors over the bed. No tall file cabinets on wheels near a glass window on an upper floor of a tall building. Take your dog for a walk around the neighborhood. Have some water and food where you know its location and how to dig it out if necessary. Don't advertise your food and water or cash before the quake, or during, or after. Share when it is the right time to share.

If you watch earthquake prediction videos, you know there is no way to say when it will happen. You also know if you live in active areas it will happen. A great big earthquake and several other great big earthquakes are coming. They will affect huge populations in many big cities in the US and other parts of the world. Be ready for an early morning quake or a mid afternoon quake or a nighttime shaker. Prepare.

When the shaking starts stay away from elevators and underground parking areas. Exit by the stairs. Bricks will fall. Electric overhead wires will fall. Chimneys will fall.

An investment in protective clothing could be helpful. Bicycle helmets and hard hats and boots and gloves, for example. Take the threat seriously. You and I will not be sleeping through a nearby 7.5 magnitude or greater quake.

Last but not least, have some extra dog and cat food.

ABOUT THE AUTHOR

Tom Willett lived in Southern California a total of slightly more than thirty years. He felt one big earthquake and about a dozen moderate quakes and many hundreds of aftershocks of various magnitudes. He knew people who had a lot of damage in the 1994 Northridge quake. Tom lived in a mobile home in Van Nuys when that earthquake struck. It was a very violent shaking felt over many square miles. The only damage in Tom's home was one broken light bulb. The items that fell out of the refrigerator were cleaned off and put back inside. Tom was very prepared for the ground motion. He was dressed and outside in about three minutes.

Tom began to make plans to move. It took a few years. Tom left California in 2006. He now lives in Tennessee. His reason for the long wait was because he was an actor and he needed a few more years of work to get his retirement credits. He did start his plan for leaving LALALand immediately after the big 1994 quake.

Tom is an entertainer who loved living in Los Angeles and Hollywood. He felt a need to write some warning words and some words of comfort for anyone who lives in a high risk area. Tom has been a movie extra, musician, actor, comic, radio announcer and writer for many decades.

Tom is not a geologist or scientist. He does not work for the USGS or any government agency. Tom is a person who had the great idea of leaving a highly populated area that expects a big earthquake of 7.5 magnitude or greater. Tom was lucky to live in Southern California when the earthquakes were usually small and moderate. Tom does not want to be in Southern California or the San Francisco area when the next huge earthquake happens. He does not want to be in Memphis or Saint Louis when the next New Madrid Fault quake occurs. Also coming sometime will be the great killer events with West Coast volcanoes and the Pacific Northwest earthquakes and tsunamis.

Tom has videos at YouTube where his name is Featureman. He has some videos that show some of the damage from the 1994 earthquake.

www.ingramcontent.com/pod-product-compliance
Lightning Source LLC
Chambersburg PA
CBHW071315280526
45788CB00004B/1907